Prophecy for Beginners

Experiments, Instructions, Examples and Models

Contact: www.HarryEilenstein.de
Harry.Eilenstein@web.de
Harry Eilenstein at youtube

Production and publishing house: BoD – Books on Demand, Norderstedt

ISBN: 9783753453750

Table of Contents

I   The Nature of Time

It is not absolutely necessary to understand the nature of time in order to develop the seer gift, but it is quite beneficial. Even if one already possesses the seer gift, sooner or later one will probably wonder what time actually is.

Therefore, this book begins with a consideration of time from different points of view.

I 1.   The view of the natural sciences on time

From the point of view of the natural sciences, time has been regarded until about 100 years ago as a uniform movement which runs continuously and always equally fast from the past to the future at all places. The only access to time is the present – the past and the future are beyond our grasp.

Time was and is the central standard in natural sciences: Natural sciences describe the change of systems in the course of time. The regularities of these temporal changes are described by natural laws. The processes themselves are called "causal" – meaning changes in the course of time according to the known rules.

There are only a few exceptions of physical measuring results which do not describe temporal changes like e.g. the constants of nature and the conservation laws.

Since the discoveries of Einstein, however, the ideas about time have changed fundamentally.

Before Einstein time was like a steady flowing river, like a straight line, like a constant, which is completely independent from everything else.

Since Einstein it is clear that time is firmly connected with space: as the three space dimensions (length, width, height) are firmly connected with each other, also time is firmly connected with space.

As long as one considers only something spatial, one can always indicate the distance of two space points as a length. If, however, time is firmly connected with space, the distance between two space/time points must also contain the element of time. The simplest connection of space and time and at the same time the only constant connection of the two is velocity: It results from the distance covered in a certain time. Thus, the distance between two space/time points is a velocity.

So far this all sounds quite "normal" – and at low velocities also everything remains quite "normal". The unusual thing about this connection of space and time is the fact that the time which passes for somebody depends on how fast somebody moves. If somebody stays on the earth and for him one year passes, for somebody who flies with a rocket at a very high speed less time passes: If he returns to the earth, for him e.g. only 11 and not 12 months have passed.

This is a strange effect in space-time: the faster you go, the less time passes. If one approaches the speed of light, finally almost no more time passes. The more you approach the speed of light, the more energy you have to spend for the next 100 kilometers per hour you want to go even faster.

But actually everybody knows this effect: "movement keeps you young" …

There is a not very precise analogy to this: If one goes from a certain point to the coast in the west, the time one needs depends on the direction in which one starts: straight to the west is fastest, to the southwest takes more time, to the south-southwest takes even considerable more time. Although you walk with the same speed, but you get different distances to the west depending on the direction. Finally, one hardly makes any progress if one walks almost due south and only 1° to the west.

Why is the speed of light such a limit? First of all it is a speed and the speed is the measure of everything in space-time.

Furthermore one could say that for the light obviously no time passes – after all it moves with the speed of light. The light stands therefore outside of time – this is an extremely important statement for a consideration of the possibility to see the future. If one would be light, one could see the whole of time, because light is timeless. The light looks, so to speak, from the outside or from above on space-time.

Einstein stated still something even more strange. His famous formula "$E=mc^2$" says that mass consists of energy. Thereupon one has been able to construct among other things atomic bombs which transform mass into energy – this formula is therefore extremely real.

If one looks at this formula more exactly, it shows that the "c^2" is the transformation item between mass and energy.

There is a fundamental difference between mass and energy: mass can be touched, it has a boundary and there can only be one mass at a given place – energy, on the other hand, cannot be touched, it has no boundary and several energies (e.g. light rays) can be at one place at the same time without interfering with each other.

This shows that the "c^2" has something to do with the "firmness" of matter. The formula "$E=mc^2$" states that energy shrinks by the factor "c^2" when it becomes matter. So this "c^2" is the transformation factor which creates matter out of energy. Since the "c" is the speed of light, this means that energy moves twice with the speed "c" – which matter does not do any more. So it is obvious to imagine that these two velocities of energy, which are lost during the transformation into matter, become tiny circular paths of energy inside the matter particles.

Matter, i.e. particles with mass, are energy spheres in which the energy no longer

5

expands with the speed of light, but moves with the speed of light (c^2) on a circular path or on a spherical surface.

The factor is "c^2" and not "c^3" or "c^1", for a sphere is a plane, i.e. it has a lenght and a breadth – the legth is one of these two "c" in "c^2" and the breadth is the other "c" in this "c^2". They are "c^2" and not e.g. "2c" because the sphere is a plane, which is calculated „lenght·breadth" thus „c^2".

In today's physics, energy quanta and matter particles are described as curvatures of space-time. An energy quantum is therefore a quality of space-time. Space-time is like a large plateau, on wich little hills and some mountains rise – the suns, planets and moons in our universe.

Space-time is therefore the actual essence of our world. If one understands space as a snapshot of space-time, time is the ultimate substance of our world. Time is therefore more than what it seems to be at first.

All substance consists of atoms – all atoms consist of elementary particles – all elementary particles consist of energy quanta – all energy quanta are curvatures of space-time – space is a snapshot of space-time – so time must be an aspect of the unity which underlies all existing ... and which itself is "timeless", since it comprises the past, the present and the future.

It is obviously this unity into which one must enter in order to be able to see the future.

In the last but one section the matter particles have been described as energy which moves on a circular path or on a tiny spherical surface – and thereby attains its "solidity". Energy acquires this intensity and outwardly its "firmness", because it becomes so to speak a laser beam, which moves on a tiny circular track. In this way Energy becomes matter.

These tiny circular paths also appear in superstring theory, which is the physical theory commonly used today to describe the world. This superstring theory is an eleven-dimensional mathematical model consisting of the time dimension, of the three "normal" extended space dimensions, and of seven tiny and therefore in everyday life invisible space dimensions – just the circular paths of energy in matter particles.

These considerations become even more exciting if one looks at black holes. These black holes are formed in the centers of galaxies, if there a star has become so large that its mass develops such an enormous gravity that not even the light can fly away from it. If this happens, the star collapses and becomes a very little sphere.

Since no light can escape the enormous gravity of such a star, such a star is "black" – it emits no light. Moreover, it becomes a "hole" – it swallows everything that comes near it and does not let it go away again. So it has been named "black hole".

There is a distance from the star, from which everything falls into the black hole without any possibility to escape. This distance is the same on all sides and consequently has the shape of a spherical surface with the giant star in its center: the so-called "Schwarzschild radius". The gravity of a black hole is so great that it pulls the entire mass of the star down to almost a very little sphere.

The formation of a black hole repeats on a large scale what happens on a small scale when a particle of matter is formed from energy:

1. encapsulation
- Energy encapsulates into matter;
- Matter encapsulates into a black hole.

2. "c^2"
- In the transformation of energy to matter, a "c^2" is lost;
- in the transformation of matter to a black hole also a "c^2" is lost.
=> At the transformation of energy into a black hole a "$c^2 \cdot c^2$" is lost, thus a "c^4". This "c^4" is the central element in the physical description of black holes.

3. velocity
- Energy moves freely with "c" in space.
- Matter moves in space with a velocity less than "c".
- In a black hole, all matter and energy collapse to one a very little sphere – consequently, there is almost no motion and no more velocity left. Motion and velocity are close to 0.

4. circular path
- Energy moves inside matter particles with "c" on a sphere.
- Mass moves first on a sphere around the center of a black hole before it falls into this center.

5. time
- Energy moves with "c", i.e. it is timeless.
- Mass moves in time at speeds less than "c".
- A black hole has such a large gravitation that it completely encapsulates the space-time around it – like this happens in a similar way with the formation of a mass particle from energy. This means that inside a black hole, time as we know it also no longer exists.

The formation of mass from energy is an encapsulation, at which the energy loses a degree of its freedom – the free movement with "c". For it it receives a firmness which energy does not have. Moreover, energy loses its timelessness – so it becomes solid and a particle moving slowly in time.

Also the formation of a black hole from mass is an encapsulation, at which the mass loses a degree of freedom – the free movement with a velocity which is smaller than "c". In exchange, it acquires an almost point-like nature that mass does not have. In addition, the mass loses its movement in the time – it becomes almost point-like, a point resting outside of time.

One can also ask oneself, what time was before the big bang. In the beginning our universe was a point, a "singularity". Does time exist in a point as we know it from everyday life? That is at least very doubtful. At least it can be said that time as we know it from everyday life has begun only with the big bang.

- - -

From these considerations it results that time is not what one normally thinks what it is:

1. Time is part of space-time. Space and time are firmly connected with each other.

2. For energy quanta like e.g. the light (photon) there is no time as we know it from the everyday life. They are timeless.

3. Also for a black hole the "normal time" does not exist any more, because it has encapsulated space-time around itself and isolated itself from it.

4. Time is an aspect of a unity, from which the whole world has originated: time $\rightarrow$ spacetime $\rightarrow$ space curvatures = energy quanta $\rightarrow$ elementary particles $\rightarrow$ atoms $\rightarrow$ world …

5. "Normal time" exists only for matter (mass), but not for the energy and also not for black holes.

6. "Normal time" arises only if energy gives up the timelessness of light and becomes mass. Mass loses this "normal time" if it gets into a black hole.

From the view of light there is only the eternity – "normal time" exists only from the view of matter. To be able to see the future, one must obviously "become light" and reach the unity which is the basis of the whole world. For this one must give up again the encapsulation, by which energy becomes matter.

These three points are a first indication of what one must do in order to be able to perceive the future:

     1. One has to become "light" (whatever this may mean concretely – probably a kind of "becoming active in the realm of consciousness");

     2. reach the Unity (almost all seers travel to the otherworld to the ancestors and gods to get their information); and

     3. to give up the encapsulation as an isolated individual being.

I 2.   The view of astrology on time

The conceptions of time in astrology look distinctly different from those in physics – at least at first glance. These ideas differ in at least two points.

The first point refers to the way of looking at Time:

Astrology does not look at temporal processes, but at simultaneities – which naturally results in a completely different picture of time. In physics one looks at what happens when, for example, two balls collide with each other – that is a temporal development. In astrology, on the other hand, one looks, for example, at the correspondence of the planetary position at the time of the birth of a person with the character of this person.

From the statement that the planetary position at the time of birth and the character of a person coincide, it follows that things do not develop individually and isolated from each other, but that the world develops as a whole. The individual parts of the world change in harmony with each other, in analogy with each other, parallel to each other – the parts of the world are organic parts of a whole. And these parts are self-similar in terms of their quality – all parts have the same quality at the same time.

This is ultimately the same conclusion that was reached when we looked at light: The world is a unity and time is an aspect of this unity, which appears in our everyday life as multiplicity.

From the astrological point of view it results in addition that the parts of the unity, thus our everyday life multiplicity form an organic whole, whose parts are all self-similar. We could also say that the multiplicity has a common rhythm in all its parts and that the whole "breathes" in the same way in all its parts at the same time.

The second point refers to the fixedness of time:

A horoscope is calculated at the time of the cutting of the umbilical cord, that is, at the time when a human being becomes physically independent. However, babies at birth have different facial features, different physiques, and different characters, which can be seen already in the mother's womb (much kicking, often turning, very quiet, reacting to noises, etc.). These characteristics coincide with the horoscope.

Thus, the characteristics of the human being are already determined before birth – they are only become astrologically visible by the time and place of birth. This means that the horoscope is already fixed before birth, but becomes calculable only from birth.

From this it follows that the time of birth is already fixed before birth, because how else could the character correspond to the horoscope? So the time as a whole is predetermined, the future is already fixed.

The same can be found in the foundation of a company: The pre-history of the foundation of the company determines what this company will ultimately become – but astrologically the character of the company becomes visible only at the moment when the foundation deed or similar is signed. Here, too, what becomes astrologically visible through the founding horoscope is already determined before the founding.

This agrees with the fact that the world is a unity and that there exixts nor time for light – the time which we experience in the everyday life exists only "below" the speed of light and only "above" the black holes.

This means for the prediction of the future that one must "step out of time" to be able to see the future. At the same time, one should be able to see the past with the same procedure.

I 3. Time on the Kabbalistic Tree of Life

The Tree of Life graphic from the Kabbalah is a structure with 11 fixed points ("Sephiroth") divided into five areas and connected by 22 lines ("paths"). This structure corresponds to the Tree of the World in the myths and was originally used by mystics to gain an experience of God.

However, the Tree of Life is a structure that is not arbitrary, but logical – similar to mathematics, although based on different principles. Just as mathematics can be used to describe all things, the Tree of Life structure can be used to describe all things. It can be found in all things – from the structure of a vacuum cleaner or a car to the structure of a cell or a human being to the German constitution or Einstein's theory of relativity.

Because all things contain the structure of the Tree of Life, one can compare all things from their structure with each other and therefore transfer knowledge from one area into other areas. (A detailed description may be found in my book "Blüten des Lebensbaumes I, II, III").

The application of the Tree of Life that is interesting in relation to the subject of this book is the exact correspondence of the Tree of Life with the superstring theory. The Tree of Life has eleven sephiroth and the superstring theory has eleven dimensions. The qualities of the eleven Sephiroth are well known through the possibilities of finding this structure in all things. If one compares the Sephiroth with the qualities of the mathematical dimensions of the superstring theory, an interesting picture emerges:

first Sephirah ("Kether"):
unity, big bang singularity, time, God.
first dimension:
time

the first triad of Sephiroth ("Chokmah", "Binah", Da'ath"):
deities, expansion of the universe, quanta of energy, without boundaries
the first triad of dimensions:
the three "normal" extended space dimensions

the second triad of Sephiroth ("Chesed", "Geburah", Tiphareth"):
soul, elementary particles
the second triad of dimension:
tiny space dimensions (smaller than an electron)

the third triad of Sephiroth ("Netzach", "Hod", Yesod"):
  psyche, atoms and molecules
the third triad of dimension:
  tiny space dimensions (smaller than an electron)

the eleventh sephirah ("Malkuth"):
  things of everyday life, multiplicity, concretization
the eleventh dimension:
  dimension which summarizes the other ten dimensions

Here we find in both systems the same division into "origin/unity – one limitless triad – two delimited triads – result/multiplicity".

The exact difference between the second and third group is not described here in more detail, since this would be quite some hassle and since this is of no importance for further considerations.

The interesting point in this comparison is that time generally corresponds to unity and origin, which in a spiritual-religious context would be called "God". This confirms the assumption that time is not just one element of the physical world among many, but that it is the core, the origin, the essence, the underlying unity of everything in the world.

More precisely, time is the experience of a succession of different states of oneness. From the point of view of unity, everything exists simultaneously; from the point of view of a part of the multiplicity, however, there is a juxtaposition (space) and a succession (time).

One can express this also a little more poetically: Time itself is timeless …

For the foreseeing of the future one can conclude from this that one must at least approach this unity with his consciousness in order to be able to see the future.

I 4. Time in the different epochs

In the different epochs of human history there have been quite different conceptions of time. The consideration of these ideas can help to make one's own ideas about time a little more "elastic".

In the **Paleolithic Age**, the idea about time will have been "point-like", as it is with today's primitive peoples: life in the here and now, which is the only thing that is real.

From this point of view every moment stands for itself. Time is nothing other than the present.

This gives rise to presence.

In **Neolithic times**, time was seen as a cycle, that is, as the repetition of an eternal rhythm: the course of the sun, the seasons, the succession of birth, life and death, and the like. Time is a cycle that repeats itself over and over again.

From this point of view, all situations in a moment are related to each other and each phase of a cycle is related to the same phase of all other cycles.

This creates a world view full of magical and astrological connections.

In the **epoch of kingship** there is a time opposition: on one side the eternity of God, the souls and the ideas and on the other side the transitoriness of the world, the body and all creations.

From this point of view only eternity is the real – the temporal is transient and therefore void.

Thereby arises the realization of a unity, which underlies all multiplicity.

In **materialism**, time is seen as a straight line along which all things develop – this is the "classical" scientific concept of time.

From this point of view, time is not a connection, but appears only as the individual movements of the individual things.

This gives rise to the knowledge of the causal, i.e. time-related, behavior of each individual thing in this world.

In the **era of globalization**, the theory of relativity and the superstring theory were discovered, which showed that time is an integral part of the world and that, among other things, the speed with which it passes depends on the speed with which that which is observed moves.

From this perspective, time is an aspect of the underlying unity of everything, which appears from the perspective of mass, thus also from the perspective of people.

This creates an integration of the previous four perspectives from which time has been viewed.

I 5.   Time in Magic

In a book about future vision, the role that time plays in magic is, of course, of great importance. In the following, however, not all known magical phenomena and models will be considered, but only those from which something can be gleaned for the understanding of time in connection with foresight.

I 5. a)   Omens and Oracles

An omen is a striking event that announces a following event that has the same quality. The omen is therefore a picture of something that is yet to come. Usually an omen refers to the near future.

For example, a hawk that catches a mouse only a few meters away from you can announce an imminent attack on you.

However, there are also complex and very detailed omens.

An omen can be described ("explained") by the fact that all events at a certain time have the same quality (like in astrology).

In an oracle, one asks a question and then uses a system of elements such as the Tarot cards, the yarrow stalks of the I Ching, or the like, to get the answer. The elements of this system represent the whole world – which is why they are a mirror of the world. Therefore, oracles can answer the question asked – they reflect the state of the world on the subject in question.

Also with an oracle an analogy is used – however not like with the omen the analogy between all things at a certain time (everything has the same quality at a certain time), but the analogy between the world and a picture of the world. The oracle is a "mirror of the world".

The oracle has the advantage over the omen that you can ask more specific questions and take the initiative yourself. The omen has on the other hand the advantage that one can receive warnings, if one pays attention to "unusual events" – even if one does not expect anything threatening.

There is another mixed form of omen and oracle: Sometimes "strange coincidences" answer you when you have asked yourself or the world a question with sufficient intensity.

I 5. b) Astrology and Physics

Physics describes the temporal development of situations – astrology describes the quality in all things at a certain point in time. Since both can be proved with certainty, the world must contain both structures: the causal relations of physics and the analogous relations of astrology.

From this it follows that the world must be a complex pattern in which everything is related to everything else and unfolds, so to speak, symmetrically like a mandala or a kaleidoscope. Otherwise the preservation of an analogical order unfolding and transforming itself uniformly in everything could not be explained.

If the world contains these two orders (causality and analogy), there have to be elements which appear in both orders – finally both orders describe the same world. This is in fact the case:

> The basic element of physics is the superstring – the basic building block of the superstring theory. Every energy quantum and every elementary particle can be represented as a superstring. A superstring is like a circularly stretched string that vibrates. This string is divided into twelve parts, i.e. it has twelve vibrations which are sharply delineated from each other.

> The basic element of astrology is the zodiac. It is also a circle consisting of twelve areas that are sharply delineated from each other.

> The qualities of the astrological aspects have the same quality as the corresponding angles in physics:

> $0°$ = conjunction = gravitation => contraction.

> $180°$ = opposition = the two poles (+ and –) of the electromagnetic force => opposition complementation

> $120°$ = trigon = the three poles of the color force => fixed connection

> $90°$ = square = separation of electric and magnetic wave in a photon (both waves are in a $90°$ angle to each other) => separation

> $60°$ = sextile = several moons in the distance of $60°$ each in the same orbit; honeycombs; snowflakes; arrangement of protons and neutrons in an atomic nucleus etc. => grouping of equal elements

> (I have described these connections in detail in my book "The Synthesis of Physics and Magic").

These angles can be derived from the zodiac (see my book "Astrologie").

The eleven mathematical dimensions of the superstring theory are not found in astrology, but in the Kabbalah (as already described).

So astrology and physics describe two aspects of the same world:

From the point of view of physics it results that time "flows" causally.

From the point of view of astrology it results that all things have the same quality at a certain time. The components of the world stand thus in a firm relation to each other, from which a large, all-encompassing pattern results. In this pattern, the twelve-divided circle as well as the angles obviously play a major role.

For the consideration of time in this book this shows that time is not only a "line" along which things move, but that every single point of time also has a certain quality.

I 5. c) Unity and Multiplicity

An important concept in many forms of magic is the opposition of unity and multiplicity: God and world in religion, Kether and Malkuth in the Kabbalah, the Tao and the Hexagrams in the I Ching, and so on. This way of looking at things corresponds to the world view of the epoch of kingship, from which philosophy also originates.

The unity is connected with the timeless eternity and the multiplicity with the "normal time".

Here the same picture is found, which has also arisen with the consideration of the difference between energy (light) and matter: Light is timeless, matter (mass) moves in time.

I 5. d) Consciousness and Matter

One of the most general definitions of magic is "the influencing of matter by consciousness".

One could say quite simply that matter is the outside of the world and consciousness is its inside.

According to this definition all things would have a consciousness – the complexity of the contents of this consciousness would then depend on the complexity of the material form to which this consciousness belongs.

A second conclusion would be that matter acts on consciousness and consciousness acts on matter – this would have to be so if matter and consciousness are two sides of the same thing. The direct perception by consciousness without the help of the physical sense organs would be telepathy and the direct acting by consciousness without the help of the physical body would be telekinesis.

If one looks at matter, it appears as single elements: stones, cells, molecules, atoms … The consciousness, however, tends to the unity: consciousness – telepathy – collective subconsciousness – God.

Consciousness is apparently connected with the timeless unity aspect of the world and matter with the time-evolving multiplicity aspect.

I 5. e)   Freedom and Inertia

If consciousness is ultimately a unity, then it is free – for what should be able to influence a unity beside which there is nothing second? This freedom appears in magic as the possibility of influencing matter by consciousness.

If matter is a multiplicity, then it is unfree – the many elements of this multiplicity brake each other in what comes out as impulse from themselves. Multiplicity is therefore "inert". This inertia appears in physics as causality: As long as consciousness does not "interfere" in the course of things, the behavior of material things develops in a predictable way.

Thus, it seems as if the consciousness looks from the timeless realm of unity into the realm of matter, which is characterized by temporal processes, and now and then intervenes in a formative way.

These last two topics, i.e. I 5. d) and I 5. e), I have presented in detail in "Magic Research for Beginners".

I 6. Summary

The results so far show that time is not simply a "straight line" along which events unfold, but has many properties – time is clearly different from what is normally imagined.

1. The amount of time that passes for a thing depends on how fast it is moving.

2. The faster something moves, the less time passes for that thing. When the speed of light is reached, no more time passes – but this speed can only be reached by light or, more generally, by quanta of energy. Light is consequently "timeless". Matter cannot reach the speed of light and therefore always remains "in time".

3. Classical physics considered time as a straight line along which the events unfold. The descriptions of this temporal development led to the concept of causality: Every state arises inevitably according to certain laws from the state preceding it – thus everything is already determined.

4. In modern physics space and time are firmly connected to each other to "space-time". The distance between two points is therefore not a distance (change of the place), but a velocity (change of the place within a certain time).

5. The time-bound mass arises from the timeless energy by compression and encapsulation of the energy: "$E=mc^2$". Thereby the energy loses twice the light velocity – more exactly it takes the "c^2" into itself whereby it becomes an "inner velocity", a rotating of the energy inside of the matter particle by which this matter particle then appears as "solid".

6. When a black hole forms, the matter particles lose again two light velocities (c^2) and become almost points – they have as part of a black hole almost no more spatial extension.

7. Matter consists of molecules; these consist of atoms; these consist of elementary particles; these consist of energy quanta; these are curvatures of space-time; space is a snapshot of space-time; thus time is the origin and the essence and the substance of the world. Time itself includes the past, the

present and the future and is therefore eternal, "temporally complete" and consequently itself a timeless entity.

8. The circular path, in which energy moves in a matter particle, are described in the superstring theory by the seven non-extended space dimensions, which exist only far below the size of an electron.

9. When matter is formed out of energy, the energy loses its timelessness and becomes a matter particle which moves in time.

10. Time has originated only when matter has formed shortly after the big bang out of energy. Only from this time on (end of the phase of the "inflationary universe") therefore also today's laws of nature began which limit e.g. the expansion of the universe to less than the speed of light.

11. Physics considers "developments in the time"; astrology considers the quality existing in "everything at a certain time". The directions of view of both approaches and consequently also their observation results are therefore completely different: Physics considers causalities, astrology considers analogies.

12. Since physics and astrology look at the same world, there are elements in both systems that are in agreement:

      - the physical angles and the astrological aspects, and

      - the twelve-part superstring and the twelve-part zodiac,

as well as:

      - the eleven-part superstring theory and the eleven-part Tree of Life of the Kabbalah.

13. From the observations of physics, which describe the causal changes in the world, and from the observations of astrology, which describe the analogies in the world, a picture of a world arises, which unfolds temporally according to fixed laws, but at the same time preserves an order of analogy. Thus, the world unfolds like a complex mandala or like a kaleidoscope – all things are related to all other things in this world in their temporal development. So the world is a complex pattern with a complex order – otherwise it could not be ordered by causality and by analogies at the same time.

14. Since the horoscope for a certain time and a certain place in the future is already fixed, also the "analogy quality", i.e. the "astrological quality" of the future is already fixed. From this it follows that the development of the world in the course of time is already fixed. Time unfolds therefore not freely, but according to fixed rules.

15. Time has been understood in different ways in the history of mankind:

- Paleolithic: point (here and now).

- Neolithic: endless cycle (circle)

- Kingship: eternity and transience (God and world)

- Materialism: time-line (causality)

- Globalization: space-time (continuum)

16. The analogies of astrology are also found in omens and oracles. They are also used in magic.

17. Consciousness is the inside of the world, matter is the outside of the world. Consciousness is free unity, matter is inert multiplicity. The intervention of free consciousness in the inert, causal processes in multiplicity is magic.

II Time Phenomena

The previous general observations of the nature of time form the basis and the framework of the following chapters.

II 1. Past, Present and Future

From the human point of view, time has three clearly distinguishable aspects:

1. the present: This is the place in time where one is at the moment, where one can perceive and act and experience.
Consciousness is first of all at this place in time, that is, in the present.

2. the past: This is the part of time that one can partially remember – the places in time where one used to be.
The consciousness can extend "backwards" in time and remember earlier events.

3. the future: This is the part of time that one cannot normally remember because one has not yet been there.
Consciousness expands into the future when looking into the future in order to see what will happen in the future.

It is conceivable that the processes of seeing the future becomes clearer if one looks more closely at the processes of remembering. Of course, especially those processes are interesting in which the memory reaches back to the time before the things one has experienced oneself.

II 1. a) Past Telepathy

The perception of past things, which one has not experienced oneself, would be so to speak "time telepathy". If someone knows about things which he has not experienced himself and about which he has not read anything, the minimal assumption would be that the person concerned has obtained the information telepathically – from a book or by the perception of a present place or the like. Even if one finds a hidden treasure in this way, one can still interpret this as "normal telepathy".

If someone can recognize complex connections in the past in this way, which one has to reconstruct laboriously when checking, the interpretation as "normal telepathy" becomes gradually difficult and "temporal telepathy" more probable: The explanation would be easier, if you say, that this person has seen the past.

II 1. b) Reincarnation

Reincarnation ultimately states that the essence of one person's life is transferred to the life of a second person who is born after the first person has died. This could also be described as "telepathy into the future" from the first person's point of view and as "telepathy into the past" from the second person's point of view.

There are many cases of people who can remember the lives of previous people, which makes either "past telepathy" or reincarnation likely.

However, the detailed consideration of this subject is quite complex and would go beyond the scope of this book (if wanted, see my book "Reincarnation").

The interesting point for the topic of this book, i.e. "future perception", is that the perception of events at a time before the perceiving person even was born, seems to be quite widespread.

II 1. c) The Collective Subconsciousness

If one has often experienced telepathy, one will assume at some point that telepathy is going on all the time, but that one is consciously aware of it only from time to time. Telepathy may also show up, for example, in the many "meaningful coincidences" in one's life.

The experiments with telepathy show that it originates in the subconsciousness. So it is not necessary to learn telepathy itself, but only to learn the perception of telepathy, i.e. the perception of one's own subconsciousness. This can be done by pendulums, dream journeys, tarot cards, family constellations, some forms of meditation, etc: One establishes a conscious connection between one's waking consciousness and one's subconsciousness.

If telepathy is the communication between the subconscious mind of a person with the subconscious mind of another person, then obviously the subconscious minds of people are telepathically intertwined. This network of subconsciousnesses and telepathic connections between them is called "collective subconsciousness".

If there should be also "temporal telepathy" (which is probable), then also the subconsciousness of a today's person could be connected with the subconsciousness of a person who lived 200 years ago. If this telepathic connection has a greater firmness and permanence and the life of the deceased person has a greater influence on the still living person, this would best be called "reincarnation". The telepathic message that reaches from the deceased person to the living person would then be the karma. In this karma would be presumably above all the more intensive experiences of the deceased: love relationships, friendships, abilities, traumas …

This is now a plausible model, which summarizes several phenomena, but still no proof for the existence of a "past telepathy". For this, the following consideration is still necessary.

II 1. d) Lycopodium

Lycopodium is a small herb that grows mainly at the edges of forests. The homeopathic remedy "Lycopodium" has been prepared from it. It is especially suitable for curing a certain form of depression: the feeling of living in the credits of one's own movie, the feeling that one's great time is already over and that all one can do is keep up a little justice. The typical Lycopodium patient is an elderly notary without a family.

The Lycopodium plants have been the most important plant species on earth 300 million years ago – the Lycopodium was the "king of the forests" at that time, because almost all the trees there belong to the Lycopodium plants. From these trees, which at that time after their death fell into the swamps, in which they partly grew, the hard coal, the oil and the natural gas were formed.

So, the small lycopod today lives on the mass graves of its "glorious ancestors". This is exactly the impression that can be found in the application of this homeopathic remedy.

Obviously, Lycopodium has a species memory that extends beyond the individual plant. One could also call this the collective subconsciousness of Lycopodium. A patient makes telepathic contact with this collective Lycopodium subconsciousness by ingesting a Lycopodium globule.

This principle, that the mode of action of a homeopathic remedy depends on the history of the substance from which this remedy has been prepared (and not on the chemical components of this substance), is also found in some other "globules".

For example, Silicea promotes slowness and thoroughness, transparency, sincerity and integration. Silicea is made from rock crystal, which is formed when SiO_2 trapped in hot lava cools extremely slowly – only 1° in a hundred years. Then the silica becomes a single molecule in which all atoms are bonded to all other atoms – a rock crystal is a single molecule. Rock crystal is thus formed slowly and all its atoms have been fully integrated into a single molecule – which is why rock crystal is transparent. This formation of rock crystal corresponds exactly to the homeopathic qualities of rock crystal.

Homeopathic remedies work by the fact that the patient, by taking "globules", enters into a telepathic connection with the collective subconsciousness of the substance from which these globules are have been made – this is, so to speak, a "magic contract" with this remedy.

From the level of the direct perception of these different collective subconsciousnesses on dream journeys or in visions, these collective subconsciousnesses of the homeopathic remedies are the "mother goddesses" of the animal species, the "elves" of the plants and the "dwarfs" of the minerals.

These collective subconsciousness beings, which one could also call "animal gods", "plant gods" and "mineral gods" or in the linguistic usage of C.G. Jung "archetypes", become naturally substantially more alive by own experiences with them e.g. on dream journeys.

These collective subconsciousnesses have obviously a "temporal extension" far into the past or differently formulated, they have a pronounced "temporal telepathy" – they can remember even their first beginnings.

This memory obviously does not depend on a physical structure but is merely an information in the collective subconsciousness of the species of animal, plant or stone. You can't call a "telepathic process" (like in "thought reading"), but you could call it a "telepathic structure".

II 1. e) Summary

The above considerations show that a "temporal telepathy" is not only possible, but also exists constantly on a large scale and embeds the individual humans, animals, plants and minerals into a collective consciousness of the respective species. This collective subconsciousness of a species corresponds to the mother goddess of man.

From the reflections on time made in "Chapter I" of this book, it appeared that light is timeless and that there is a plane in the world which is timeless and a unity and closely connected with consciousness.

Obviously, the collective subconsciousnesses of the different species stand at the transition between matter and consciousness, at the transition between multiplicity and unity, and at the transition between time and timelessness:

1. These collective subconsciousnesses have a multiplicity of independent bodies (e.g., all lycopod plants) and they have a collective subconsciousness that contains the memory of the entire species. This can also be called "temporal telepathy".

2. These collective subconsciousnesses stand between unity and multiplicity, since they combine the multiplicity of, for example, the individual Lycopodium plants into the collective subconsciousness of Lycopodium, that contains the memories of all Lycopodium plants.

3. These collective subconsciousnesses are independent of the passage of time and contain, for example, in the case of Lycopodium, memories of over 300 million years. The collective Lycopodium subconsciousness is on the one hand "in time" because it is associated with each Lycopodium plant, but on the other hand it is also "out of time" because it spans a far greater period of time than the life span of a single plant.

The functioning of homeopathy obviously corresponds to the considerations about time from "Chapter I".

It will be this transition between matter and consciousness, between unity and multiplicity, between time and timelessness, which one must reach in order to be able to see into the future.

One can sense a hidden structure in the world when looking at the collective subconsciousnesses: Every living being, plant and mineral has its own collective subconscious – its deity, so to speak. These deities are again connected with each other and form then altogether the collective subconsciousness or the deity of the earth, which is called today often "Gaia". These planetary deities could again form parts of a solar system deity, these in turn could be part of a galaxy deity, and these finally could be parts of the all-encompassing collective subconscious, which could somewhat poetically be called "God's dream".

Viewed in front of this background, reincarnation ist just the collective subconsciousness of the incarnations of a single soul. Reincarnation is the temporal telepathy of a person to the former incarnations of his soul.

II 2.   Simultaneity

Astrology describes qualities that are found in all beings, things and events at a particular moment in time: the horoscope of that moment.

This quality of the moment can be found not only in horoscopes but also in the use of analogies in magic, in the invention of a thing by several people independently of each other at the same moment, and the like. The most striking is probably the "meaningful coincidence", which has been called "synchronicity" by C.G. Jung, i.e. "simultaneity".

II 3.   Time and Simultaneity

The combination of this simultaneity or this astrologically describable momentary quality with the collective subconsciousnesses gives an interesting picture: The different collective subconsciousnesses (species deities) move synchronously in the rhythm of the astrologically describable qualities. They move together, in analogy to each other – this could be described more poetically as the "common dance of the deities", which represents "God's dream".

It is this area at the border between God and man, between timelessness and time, between unity and multiplicity, between consciousness and matter, into which the seers travel – they contemplate the collective subconsciousness, they converse with it, they wander about in it ...

III Movements in Time

After these preparatory considerations about the nature of time, the actual fore-seeing of the future can now be examined in more detail.

III 1. Unintentional Foreseeing of the Future

Probably the most common form of foreseeing the future is the unintentional vision of the future – and of this again the nightly dreaming of the events of the following day seems to be the most widespread.

Here several things can be observed:

1. The perception of the future takes place during the dream, i.e. in the subconscious.

2. These dreams occur in many people for a while and then disappear again. For example, a school friend of mine dreamed almost every night for about three months some things, that happened the next day. After that this kind of dreams occurred only very rarely.

3. The perception of the future can happen without one's own action and without willful intention. This means that one already has the "wire" to the area where one can see the future – so this connection does not have to be established first.

4. Often completely trivial things are dreamed in advance. So no great emotions are necessary to get the foresight going. It is more like opening the door and looking what will happen in the future.

5. In most cases, what is dreamed is what will happen the next day. Apparently, the "near future" is the part of the future that can be seen most easily.

Sometimes there are cases that need to be examined more closely. For example, one night I dreamed a part of the last volume of the "Harry Potter" series before it was even published, and then told that part to a friend. Later, when the volume was published, I saw that I had really seen the first chapter of this book in my dream.

Now was this the perception of the future or was this the perception of what J.K. Rowling carried in her consciousness or maybe had already written?

It was something else, but I didn't find that out until a few years later, by chance. J.K. Rowling gave the first chapter of this volume to a homeless magazine in England before the book was published, thereby boosting the sales of that newspaper. This means that at the time of my dream many people in England read this first chapter and I, who was very eager to read the last volume, telepathically "read along".

In this case, there has been a great deal of motivation on my part and a very great deal of interest in this first chapter on the part of the readers of this chapter in the homeless magazine as well. So this is a case of telepathy that was set in motion by a great motivation and many feelings – and it was no "future telepathy".

III 2.   Intentional Foreseeing of the Future

There are a great number of different methods for the intentional foreseeing of the future.

III 2. a)   Omens and Oracles

The least active is the interpretation of omens: The omen appears, one notices it and interprets it – and possibly behaves according to it.

The omen speaks with the help of a simile – so you have to transfer this omen to your own situation with the help of an analogy. If one sees three times in a row in unusually large proximity two birds which mate, one can have the justified hope that one will experience something similar quite soon …

In an oracle one asks a question and uses a system of symbols which in their totality represent the world. The randomly selected elements of this system then give the answer to the question asked.

Again, the answer is given in a general, more or less symbolic way, which one must then apply to the question asked.

An interesting point is the "temporal range" of these two methods. With the omens, it is clear that, like the nighttime "future dreams", they almost always indicate the near future, i.e. the next day. With the oracles the "temporal range" seems to be some-what wider because of the questions asked, but the answers still refer to the "next step of development", thus ultimately also to the "near future".

III 2. b)   Astrology

In astrology, the question of time is quite different from that of omens and oracles: The point in time about which one receives a statement depends only on the point in time for which one calculates a horoscope. So now in the year 2020 A.D. one can already say exactly which character a person will have who will be born in the year 2050 A.D. in Berlin at 12.00PM. Besides the horoscope exists a life long and does not change.

Moreover, the horoscope works already before the birth and "shapes" the person concerned – the horoscope becomes only visible and calculable at the moment of the birth.

Here a different aspect of time is shown than in the omens and oracles, which almost always show the "next step". Through astrology it becomes clear that the successive qualities of time are already fixed in the future – one can always look at the horoscope belonging to any day.

The astrological quality of the "flow of time" is already fixed – even the qualities of day thousands of years in the furture.

One sees something different in the direct perception by "future dreams" and by the indirect perception with the help of omens and oracles than with the help of astrology:

- future dreams: concrete events mainly in the next day

- omens: the near future in parable form

- oracles: the next step of development in parable form

- astrology: the time quality of any point of time

While future dreams show quite concrete events in the future, omens, oracles and astrology represent the future as a quality, i.e. one must first transfer this quality to the concrete question, i.e. "interpret" the omen, the oracle or the horoscope.

III 2. c) Dream Journeys

With the help of dream journeys one can also look at the future. The simplest method is as follows:

- You formulate a question to the future: What do you want to know? To whom does the question refer? What point in time is it about?

- Then you imagine a calendar, a series of year circles, a line on which the years and months are marked or something similar, i.e. a graphical representation of time.

- Now you relate this imagined time-line to the person or subject you want to know something about.

- Finally, one travels inwardly to the date about which one wants to know something in relation to the selected topic.

Depending on the nature of the question, one must also travel along the time-line from the present month by month and see what happens in each month.

It may also be useful to wish oneself to the (as yet unknown) point of time when something specific will happen.

Another variant is to look simply in all months of the following year, what things will happen then.

One can also use an oracle like e.g. tarot cards or a hexagram from the I Ching as a "gate" for a dream journey. In this way, one can add concrete images to the oracle's answer, which, after all, consists of the representation of a quality, allowing a more concrete answer.

It can also be helpful if you do not to look into the future alone but together with several people and then compare what you have seen and what you have heard. Of course, one does not know for sure whether the matching information came about because one saw the same thing in the future or because one telepathically perceived what the others saw.

It is also not at all certain that one has not seen the future, if two or three have seen something different, because they could have seen different aspects of the future.

In any case, the picture of the future becomes richer and somewhat more certain when several people look into the future.

As with all magic experiments, it is useful to write down what you have foreseen and then compare it with the future when you arrive at it.

III 2. d)   Constellations

Family constellations are another method. Although they are traditionally meant for healing family structures, one can also use them to see the future.

The simplest method here is to determine a place in the room where the relevant point in time in the future is to be located – just as one determines before laying out tarot cards what meaning the e.g. the three places are to have where one will then lay a tarot card (e.g. root of the theme, the theme itself at the moment, further development of the theme).

Then you stand at this place, that represents the future, and see what you perceive there. What you perceive corresponds to the tarot card that you turn over at a certain place when laying the cards – but the perceptions in this "constellation method" can become quite concrete and precise with a little practice.

III 2. e) Ancestors and Gods

If you study older reports about seers and visionaries, you will notice that in many cases these seers and visionaries, while "seeing", go inwardly as if on a dream journey to the ancestors and to the gods and ask them about the future. So they go to the otherworld – which here is obviously identical with the collective subconsciousness.

In more recent times, family constellations have the same approach – you talk to the ancestors to clarify things from the past. However, one can ask them just as well about the future. From about 1850 ago until about 1960, spiritism was also well known, in which contact was made with the ancestral spirits in various ways (Quija board, etc.) in order to learn from them, among other things, about the future.

During the Christianization in Europe necromancy (evocation of the dead), with whose help one wanted to learn something from the dead among other things obout the future, fell badly into disrepute. However, in the Neolithic Age, in royalty, and probably even before that in the Paleolithic Age, contact with one's ancestors was the main source of advice and help. Shamanism, which is the oldest form of religion, is largely based on establishing this contact with the ancestors.

An alternative to contacting the ancestors is contacting the gods, who can also be consulted about the future. The method here is either the oracle (which gives symbolic quality answers) or the dream journey (which gives concrete answers).

The gods are also in the otherworld, i.e. in the collective subconsciousness.

III 2. f) The General Perception of the Future

There is also a possibility of general access to the knowledge about the future. For this purpose one has to undertake a certain dream journey. The area in which one goes can be called "karma archive", "book of destiny", "Sephiroth Chesed on the Kabbalistic Tree of Life", "Akashic Chronicle", etc.

This place has several characteristics:

  - It is located in the beyond.

  - It is in the realm of souls – which is identical with the beyond.

  - It is the area of overview in the realm of souls.

  - It is transparent, that is, you can look everywhere and see everything, when bing in this place.

34

- In it there are still delimitation, but the delimitation are "thin" and transparent.

- In it, one sees things as they are, i.e. without concealment and repression – however, one still has the choice of what one wants to see and what not.

- If you go one step further, you come to the "boundaryless place", which is called "abyss" and "Da'ath" in the Kabbalah and is called "otherworld bridge" and the like in the mythology. Here one sees all things and can no longer choose what one sees and what one does not see. Here also any delimitation dissolves – which can cause the feeling of falling into a bottomless abyss.

The essence of this inner place can best be described by a dream journey I once took with my friend Jörg, because I had come to the conclusion that in order to get along in my life, I would have to know why my soul actually decided to create such a strange Harry in this life.

Chesed is an area on the Kabbalistic Tree of Life, which is one of the areas of the "Soul Plane," which includes the "Circle of Past Reincarnations" and the "Akashic Chronicle," among others.

The dream journey began with me going back in my memory first in five-year steps and then in year steps towards birth, telling Jörg at each step where I am at the moment. Since I could already remembered my birth at that time, the way back to that point was quite easy. Jörg had only isolated, fleeting images of my life in this part and felt rather left out.

At first the perception from the time before my birth was as one would imagine it: dim light, warm, weightless, no breathing, eating or drinking of my own – rather resting and waiting.

Upon reaching the time of 4 weeks after conception, the perception changed: I was a consciousness and perception that formed a sphere (of life force) *and protruded beyond my mother's womb about 10cm.*

At 3 weeks after conception, this sphere was much larger (diameter about 1.5 m) *and the sphere seemed to revolve around its center, which was anchored in my mother's womb.*

At 2 weeks after my conception, this sphere was even larger (diameter about 4m) and my consciousness was like a sphere within this sphere on an orbit, creating a kind of vortex.

1 week after my conception this state was about the same, only the anchoring still felt very loose.

At the time of my conception, I was near my parents and could sense their feelings. I briefly wondered if this was indiscreet now, but since I was in a sense the main person in this event, I decided it was o.k. that way.

When I then returned to the time before my procreation, I saw my soul absorbed in itself in a heavy, serious, almost depressed mood and I wondered if all souls feel this way shortly before the procreation of their future body.

I had the feeling that Jörg could now come next to me, since I was now outside my memories as Harry and we were now in the familiar realm of dream travel. I asked Jörg about it and when he agreed, I sent a beam of light from me to him to mark the way to me. When the ray of light arrived at him, I had the feeling that I should give him my hand along the ray of light (only in the vision, not with my material hand) *and pull him over to me.*

During this being pulled over, Jörg had the feeling to be pulled through several pages of the Egyptian Book of the Dead.

When he was then next to me, we looked at my soul and Jörg pointed out to me that the soul is sitting here in front of a place which looks like an arena. On our questions to the arena about its nature Jörg received the answer 'preparation' and I 'place of silence' – thus a place of silent preparation of the souls for their next incarnation.

On my question to the 'place of silence' where I could receive information about my decision to lead this life, I was directed by him to a place far behind me. Jörg and I turned around and flew there. I saw a large round sphere whose surface had large streaks, as if from a slow-flowing liquid.

"Apache tear," said Jörg (=smoke obsidian).

"Fits well," I replied, "in stone healing, smoke obsidian is the stone that brings you back to what you originally once wanted. And the streaks in the surface of the sphere really do resemble the flowing lava from which the smoke obsidian is formed. – Look, there's a space inside the sphere and a seat of sorts. I'm going to go inside."

"I'll stay outside – the place is not approved for me."

"Yes, I feel that way too."

On the seat in this sphere I felt again the heaviness in the 'mind' of the soul, which I had felt in it also already at the 'place of silence'.

When I had united with my soul and was sitting there in the sphere on the seat, I could only direct my consciousness forward to the coming incarnation – apparently my soul was exclusively occupied with the decision for this incarnation while sitting on this seat in this sphere.

I did not manage to get more concrete information from it about the reason for this coming (my present) *life. However, upon my question to my soul, a kind of light rays appeared behind me on the left, pointing to the information I wanted.*

"We have to go further, Jörg, here the information does not exist yet."

We flew toward the source of this light and were surprised to see a huge, white-radiant building teeming with equally white-radiant people in and in front of it. The tower-like building was far larger than anything previously seen in man-made buil-

dings.

When we tried to enter the building, we felt that it was forbidden for us to do so.

"Only dead people are allowed to enter," said Jörg, "unless you meet certain conditions."

"What conditions?"

"I don't know."

"Who should we ask? The gatekeeper of the house?"

"Yes, that's what I was thinking."

There was a big crowd outside the gatekeeper's window and it took me a while to get to the window and ask the gatekeeper my question.

"The condition is that every living person who learns the reason for his incarnation must follow his truth."

When I shared this answer with Jörg, he agreed with me: "I received as an answer that after entering this house, the residual freedom one has due to his ignorance disappears and one is bound to his decision (to life one's current incarnation). *"*

After a short consideration I decided to accept this condition and told this to the gatekeeper, whereupon I was allowed to enter the house.

Jörg told me that he had to stay outside, but that he could see inside the house, since we had already been in this building before this time. The house had looked somewhat different then, on our earlier dream journey here to Chesed.

"It's strange how many 'dead' people there are – you don't usually realize that ... and they look more alive than the living." Jörg commented.

There were also a lot of white-glowing people in the building. I wished my way to the right place in the building and arrived in a large, high, elongated room, which reminded me of a Gothic church. In this room there was a lot of fear in the middle third (of the height).

When I looked at the front wall of the room, a large picture appeared there, making the room look like a movie theater. On the 'screen' I could see a landscape passing by that looked familiar. Then came a scene in which I could see my death in one of my past lives, of which I had already had some visions.

"Look at the walls," said Jörg, "there are faces there."

As I looked up at the side walls, I also saw these faces and I recognized them as my previous incarnations, some of which I had already seen on previous dream journeys. As I looked at them and thought how much fear there is, one of the faces corrected me: "Fear, greed and hate!"

(Thes three fundamental problems of man according to Buddhism are greed, hatred and delision.)

Somewhat perplexed, I looked around.

"This room is not only a 'cinema,' but also a 'library,'" Jörg commented.

As I pondered where in this room I could find the information about my soul's

37

intention for my present life, I sensed a large, bright, white light at the front above the *room, which Jörg could also see shining in the upper third of the building, and whose* *name I spontaneously recognized as 'Wisdom'.*

Speaking to this light was very easy and the answers came very clearly. I wished *myself to the place at which the light was. From the outside this light seemed to be* *almost endless; from the inside* (when I connected with the light) *its boundaries were* *clear. It had no inner structure, only this outer border, which one could hardly see* *from the outside.*

I said to Jörg: "I believe this light is the highest form, which a living being can *take, which is still delimited."*

When I asked this light for the desired information, it showed me a place on the *wall of the room where the light was.*

"Behind it lies the knowledge, the knowledge of your whole life."

"If I want to know the intention for my present life, does that mean I will know the *entire course of my present life?"*

"Yes."

"Um, I think I will ponder about that for a while – I'd rather not rush into that."

I thanked him and went back out to Jörg: "Knowing the entire course of my life is *quite strange after all – it completely changes your perspective."*

"Yes, then freedom disappears, just as the gatekeeper said it would."

"It rather shifts from the level of my psyche to the level of my soul."

"The apparent freedom or limited freedom during life then becomes the freedom of *the decision to live this life."*

"Well, it also fits with this: that by this knowledge one becomes bound to fidelity to *one's own truth."*

"Is there anything important to do here, Jörg, before we return? – I think there's *something up ahead on the left where we should go again."*

We came to a sort of pond or fountain surrounded by a good knee-high wall, with *another small circular wall in the middle.*

Jörg: "What is the name of the place?"

"I get 'Lake of Memories' as an answer."

"What are we supposed to do here?"

"Put our hand in it or drink from it."

"Throw a coin in it."

"So it seems to be about a symbolic contact. And it seems to be important that not *only one of us, but both of us make this contact."*

So we both bent over the water and made contact. I saw a Chinese-style dragon and *Jörg saw war scenes. As we talked about it, the two sceneries began to change.*

Jörg: "Since it seems to be important for both of us, let's go in."

"All right."

The scene immediately became clearer and we stood before a dragon that enveloped us in its fire.

"The fire signifies a blessing with strength, Jörg."

I put a hand on the dragon's scales and felt the smoothly scoured, shiny horn scales and the elongated ridges and burrs on it and said in wonder, "Funny, I've never touched a dragon before."

Then I almost had to laugh when I realized what I had said.

After a while we returned upstairs in front of the well. There we felt that it was important in this case to return exactly the same way we had come. Which we then did.

The "sphere" in which I saw myself in the first four weeks after my conception consist of the 'substance' of the psyche, that is, life force.

The "life force sphere" can be felt quite clearly in pregnant women in the first 3-4 weeks, and from this the pregnancy of the woman can be recognized.

The place of silence in this vision is called "Tiphareth" on the Tree of Life – the area of the individual soul.

The ball of smoke obsidian on the Tree of Life is called "Geburah" – the realm of karma, i.e. the soul's motivation for its current incarnation. The dragon we met on the way back also belongs to this realm.

The great building on the Tree of Life is called "Chesed" – the realm of transparency, where all information can be found. This area is sometimes called "akasha chronicle".

The akasha chronicle, i.e. the hall of memories of previous incarnations, is a detailed variant of the experience that sometimes occurs during the dream journey to one's own center: the persons who have found their own soul (Tiphareth) sometimes go further until they come to a circle of people who appear to this person like brothers and sisters (Chesed) – although only in the rarest cases it becomes immediately clear to the dream travelers that these are their figures in their own previous incarnations.

The faces on the walls of this hall were my previous incarnations.

The "dead" we saw in Chesed looked more alive than the living because they were only souls without psyches and therefore the radiance of the souls has not been dimmed by the fears, addictions and self-doubts in the psyche.

The well is the beginning of the path between Chesed and Geburah – just like the ray of light we followed from the "Apache Tear" to the "big building" to Chesed.

From the soul it is easy to look into the psyche, but from the psyche most people can only look into the realm of the soul from time to time until they are about 5 years old. After that, the border between psyche and soul remains largely opaque until one has harmonized and healed one's own psyche to the greatest possible extent.

This effect leads to the fact that although the soul can see all its previous incarnations, the waling consciousness within a single incarnation can still remember its own soul during the first five years, but after that it forgets it and can no longer see its previous incarnations. This memory is usually regained only by meditations and dream journeys.

The inner voice, which sometimes can speak very clearly to a person and usually gives the central indications in one's life, probably comes here from Chesed from the light of wisdom. This light of wisdom, that is the essence of one's own soul and all its previous incarnations, gives, so to speak, at the essential points in one's life, supporting directing instructions for the normal waking consciousness in the world – telepathy from the wisdom of the soul to the everyday waking consciousness.

I have not yet looked at the rest of my life, but presumably this will happen at some point – which means that I will then shift my center from my psyche to my soul, so that my soul will then become my identity instead of my psyche. Such a serious transformation, it seems to me, should be approached only after careful consideration and good preparation.

The being that I met on this dream journey at the "Place of Silence" and in the "Lava Sphere" and that I called "Soul" was actually the preparation of my present incarnation. My soul has been the light in the great building.

The hall of memories of the former incarnations is a detailed variant of the experience which sometimes occurs on the journey to one's own center: The people who have found their own soul sometimes go further on until they come to a circle of "luminous people" who appear to the dream traveler like brothers and sisters – although only in the rarest cases it becomes immediately clear to these dream travelers that these are the figures of their own earlier incarnations.

III 2. g)   The Sensation of Seeing the Future

The "looking into the future" feels like remembering – only in the other direction – so to say a "remembering of the future". This identity of sensation confirms that the future already exists as well as the past – the quality of a day in the past as well as the quality of a day in the future can also be described in the same way with the help of astrology.

The "looking into the future" is also connected with the same sensation as telepathy: It is a searching inner looking and inner feeling. One knows where one wants to go and focuses one's attention on that place or subject. The future vision is apparently really a "temporal telepathy".

If one does not look into the future on one's own initiative, but suddenly becomes aware of the future as in a dream or vision, this is like a sudden idea, a sudden memory, an unexpected input.

This also feels "quite normal". Therefore, at first it is not so easy to recognize a future vision – it can easily be mistaken for figments of one's own imagination.

In the case of "spatial telepathy" it helps in such a case to see whether one can see the roots of what has appeared so unexpectedly in one's own consciousness, i.e. the previous step of the thoughts or the preliminary stage of the picture which one has seen all at once. If it is an image of one's own psyche, one can find its roots; if, however, it stands isolated and without connections in one's own psyche, it is most probably a telepathic perception.

The same difference exists in "temporal telepathy", that is, in seeing the future. If one cannot see the roots of the picture and perhaps finds it completely absurd, the probability is high that it is really a future vision.

This does not mean, of course, that all the things that seem plausible must originate out of one's own psyche – the distinguishing criterion is whether one can see or feel within oneself the source of the image.

III 3.   How fixed is time?

Probably the most frequent point of discussion on the subject of "looking into the future" is the question of whether the future is already fixed or not. The fact that one can already calculate and interpret the horoscope for a person who will be born on a certain date in the future, as well as future dreams, clearly suggest that the future is already fixed.

The answer to this question aims at the heart of human self-understanding: Are we free or completely determined?

III 3. a)   Man and World

First of all, it can be stated that man has a free will even if everything is already determined. This free will would then be merely a part of what is already fixed – what man decides freely has its roots in the psyche of the person concerned. From this perspective, freedom would be the subjective perspective ("I do what I want!") and determinacy would be the objective perspective ("Everything that someone decides is rooted in that person."). In the first case the individual sees that he decides in such a way, as he wants it from his inside (thus he is free); in the second case one sees from the outside that the inner decision of the individual has its causes in himself (thus he is determined in his decision).

It is different with the practicability of the decisions – human beings are not omni-potent. However, each human being is a part of the whole and determines partly the development of the whole. The individual is a part of the flow of the events, not only an ineffective ball which is merely tossed back and forth by the other play balls. However, there are a lot of balls in this game, which limits the effectiveness of one's own ball …

If one looks from a "point of view in time" on the events, one sees that constantly someone decides something and everywhere something happens, whereby constantly unpredictable developments come into operation. If you look at what is happening from a "timeless point of view", you see the whole, the course of things – if there is no time at the point of view from which you look, things are static and fixed: things proceed as they proceed …

Seen from "outside of time" one looks at a string of pearls and can see it as a whole – seen from "in time" one jumps from one pearl to the next and does not know what comes next.

III 3. b)   Freedom and Causality

However, the question "Is everything already fixed or is it changeable?" is not yet decided by this. If the multiplicity of matter is merely inert, but not unambiguously determined and causally completely fixed, and, moreover, the unity of consciousness is free and can therefore intervene in the inertia of matter and help to shape it creatively, there is no unambiguous answer: the people, beings and things in the world are neither completely free nor completely fixed.

It depends on the independence of the consciousness how much influence it can take.

If we look at this statement more closely, we can see that the question of the nature of time still remains unanswered. Magic enables a greater overview of one's own situation and a greater control of this situation – the influence and the effectiveness of one's own decisions can be significantly increased by magic. But does this increase not originate in the person concerned? Is it not also causally originated? Is it therefore not also already fixed?

Presumably, freedom has (at least) three aspects:

1. Everyone is an effective part of the world and therefore shapes the world according to his own preferences. This effectiveness and therefore also the quality of the fruits of one's own freedom increase with the growing clarity, autonomy and independence of one's own consciousness.

2. By magic, one can significantly increase the effectiveness of one's own decisions, which does not lead to omnipotence, but allows for a previously unknown effectiveness of one's own decisions and actions.

3. The causality of matter is not absolute, but only great – matter is "inert". However, if the consciousness is clearly enough directed to a goal, magic arises, which can lead up to materializations. Because of the freedom of the consciousness and the inertia of the matter there is neither an absolute freedom nor an absolute determinacy, but the creative influence of the consciousness.

The question whether everything is already determined or everyone is free, is actually the question whether one can decide something in his consciousness and then also realize this. Here it is the question, how one defined that, after whose freedom one looks for: Is it the consciousness? The waking consciousness? Or the waking consciousness together with the subconsciousness? Or the soul? Or the everyday ego? Or the combination of waking consciousness, subconsciousness, deep sleep consciousness and ecstasy state?

Already this variety of possibilities shows that there is not the one "point" in the human being which could be free or not free – the whole is too complex for that. Besides, every component of the human psyche has also a prehistory, i.e. it has originated causally.

If you want, you can also ask the question whether you have actually decided for your your own horoscope ... Since the psyche has not yet existed before the own procreation, it can hardly have decided for the own horoscope – only one's own soul could have done that. Or is the horoscope only an external influence? That would be however an external influence which has completely coined the own being and with which one has identified oneself completely ...

The question of personal freedom cannot be answered simply. One can decide, one has influence on the events, but one has also emerged from the past and the own influence is limited. In addition, the consciousness also has the possibility of direct influence on events (magic), but this does not mean that every person is free, but only that his influence is greater than it is usually assumed in today's culture.

The question about freedom is in the end above all the question "Can I decide something and then carry it out? Or is everything already fixed and I don't even need to try?"

This questioning is a fallacy. By striving intensively for what one wants to achieve, one can achieve the best possible. It is probably already determined what one can achieve – but it is so only seen from the outside from an objective "point of view outside of time". Seen from the subjective "point of view within time" every decision also has an effect – thus one forms his own life.

Since these considerations ultimately serve to better understand the nature of "looking into the future", one can at least say that there is no clearly recognizable reason for the assumption that the course of events could not already be completely fixed.

However, in this fixed course of events there can be magical influences which contradict "normal causality". This means only that one must extend the picture of causes and effects in this "fixed flow" of the things by magic connections. The existence of magic, however, does not refute the assumption that the development of events is already completely fixed.

III 3. c)   The Perspective of the Soul

The dream journey to my soul, which I mentioned in an earlier chapter, shows that the soul and the psyche have two different perspectives on the world and also on the present incarnation. The following considerations presuppose of course that one assumes the existence of a soul – what I do not want to consider here in more detail.

The soul exists already before one's own procreation and exists also still after one's own death. For one's soul a procreation is therefore about the same as for the psyche of a human being the morning awakening – the death is for the soul about the same as the evening falling asleep. Just as a human being can effortlessly link several days together by his memory, the soul also has an overview of its successive incarnations.

If the soul decides for an incarnation, it seems to know the entire course of this incarnation – at least it offered me on my dream journey to show me the rest of my life. Since one can look even from the psyche into the future, one should be able to assume that the soul, which is closer to the unity of consciousness than the psyche, can perceive still more clearly one's own future.

So it would be obvious that one should go to one's own soul if one wants to know something about the future – especially if it is about one's own future.

The psyche strives to make the decisions that will lead to the most acceptable situations for it. But what does the soul strive for, if it has decided the incarnation ahead itself and already knows all the events in this incarnation? It cannot be the formation of this incarnation what the soul strives for, since it has already chosen and formed this incarnation and knows it completely. So it can only be about the concrete experience of that what it has decided abstractly, so to speak.

The psyche, which is as far as possible "in time", tries to take the best possible way "in time". The soul, which is at least partly "outside of time", already knows all events and only wants to experience them. This results in a division of labor between psyche and soul:

- The soul plans and decides; the psyche experiences.

- The soul is the entrepreneur; the psyche is the manager.

- The soul needs the psyche to be able to experience its decisions; the psyche needs the soul to receive orientation.

- The soul has the serene view from "outside of time"; the psyche has the view of the intense experience of events "in time."

The seeing of the future has obviously also much to do with the contact with one's own soul – or with the contact with the souls of others, whose future one tries to recognize.

III 3. d)   The House of Consciousness

"Looking into the future" is something one does with one's consciousness. So it might be helpful to look more closely at the different aspects of consciousness.

First of all, there is the <u>waking consciousness</u>, that is, the part of the consciousness that is reading these very words. In the waking consciousness there is always the information that is needed to make a meaningful decision in the current situation. So the waking consciousness is something like an "office for the current processes".

Then there is the <u>subconsciousness</u>, which one can experience at night when dreaming or also in meditations, on dream journeys, in visions, with halluzi-nationen etc.. The subconsciousness contains all memories, all inner thoughts and all other images of the psyche. They stand in it on an equal footing – as, among other things, dreams show, which do not make any moral or other selection. The subconsciousness is like a big archive, in which everything is filed and stored, which one has ever experienced, thought and felt. As, among other things, dream journeys and the possibility of remembering show, that this archive is well sorted, so one can find everything in it.

Between the office and the archive there is a door through which the infor-mation from the archive can enter the office because the archive considers it important in the current situation (inspirations, ideas, sudden memories, asso-ciations, etc.) or because the office has requested this information from the archive (remembering, dream journeys, meditation, etc.).

On the desk in the office there is a desk lamp, which can highlight particularly important things with a spotlight. When this light is turned on, the consciousness focuses on a single thing – this is the one-pointed state of <u>ecstasy</u>. The reason for turning on this "ecstasy lamp" can be fear, addiction, lust or conscious concentration as well as meditation.

Finally, there is the house, where the office, the archive and the desk lamp are located. This "house consciousness" is the <u>deep sleep consciousness</u> that can be experienced in meditation as inner stillness. This is the "consciousness in itself" in which there are no consciousness contents.

Now in the world there is more than one person, i.e. there are many "houses of consciousness" each with an archive, an office and a desk lamp in them.

- Between the waking consciousnesses of the people ("offices") there is the conscious exchange e.g. in the conversation.

Between the subconsciousnesses of the people ("archives") there are telepathic connections. This creates the <u>collective subconsciousness</u>, which is, so to speak, a "total archive" of people's experiences, in which the memories of people who lived in earlier times are also preserved.

The ecstatic consciousness is experienced by each person individually, although of course two people can be in ecstasy at the same time – e.g. during sex or in a fight to the death or also in meditation.

Then there are the many "houses of consciousness", whose silent consciousness without content together forms the "city of consciousness". Presumably this silent consciousness without contents is the "consciousness in itself", which underlies all consciousnesses.

Forms of Consciousness			
Individual Consciousness	*Contents*	*Image*	*Collective consciousness*
deep sleep (silence)	none	"house"	all-encompassing consciousness
subconsciousness (dream)	all	"archive"	collective subconsciousness
waking consciousness	those which are important in the moment	"office"	conversation
ecstasy consciousness	one	"spotlight of the desk lamp"	possibly simultaneously, but not together

The different forms of meditation are combinations of two or more forms of consciousness. The waking consciousness is always included, because meditation is a waking conscious process. According to this definition, the state of hypnosis, for example, is not meditation, because the waking consciousness of the hypnotized person has been switched off.

waking consciousness + subconsciousness	= dream journeys etc.
waking consciousness + deep sleep consciousness	= silent meditation
waking consciousness + ecstasy consciousness	= Tantra, sigel magic

When "looking into the future" it is about purposefully searched images outside of the waking consciousness. For this the combination "waking consciousness + subconsciousness" is obviously used, thus a form of the dream journey.

With the combination "waking consciousness + deep sleep consciousness" the consciousness contents are missing – and the knowledge about the future consists of information, thus in consciousness contents.

In the combination "waking consciousness + ecstasy consciousness" the attention is reduced to one single content of consciousness, which is also unsuitable for a future vision – ecstasy meditation is not a search, but a one-directed concentration.

So the previous assumption that the future vision is a "dream journey moving in time", i.e. "temporal telepathy", is quite plausible.

III 3. e)   The Chakras

One could assume that the chakras play a role in seeing the future – the chakra name "Third Eye" already sounds as if one could see into the distance and into the future with it. However, since you don't need to "turn on" your Third Eye for telepathy and dream journeys, you obviously don't need to consider the chakras separately when looking into the future.

The chakras have (very briefly) the following properties:

The Heart Chakra is the "temple of the soul" where one's identity is located – this chakra corresponds to deep sleep consciousness.

The two chakras that correspond to the subconscious are the Solar Plexus and the Throat Chakra. Therefore, they should be especially active during dreams, dream journeys, telepathy and telekinesis. It fits that life force threads ("silver cords") go from the Solar Plexus to other people and establish a telepathic connection by which life force can also flow. These life force threads can also be used in magic in many ways.

So, one could experiment with whether imagining such a life force thread to the situation in the future that one wants to see is helpful.

Hara and Third Eye are connected with the waking consciousness. Since the waking consciousness only contains already known information or recombines it and applies it to the momentary situation, these two chakras will not play a central role in seeing the future.

The Root Chakra and the Crown Chakra belong to the one-pointed ecstatic consciousness, that is, to the experience of the here and now. Since the future is not in the here and now, these two chakras will play at most a secondary role in the vision of the future.

III 4. The Risks of Seeing the Future

What happens when one has seen the future? One knows it or one tells it to others, who then know it. Then they may change their behavior and experience something different than if they had not changed their behavior because of the seer's prophecy. Thus, the seer bears part of the responsibility for the experience of the people to whom he or she predicts something.

First of all, this is quite normal – this happens also in every conversation and in every encounter.

But what about when existential questions are at stake: "Will this or that behavior keep me from dying of my disease?" – "Should I take the risk of getting Corona or am I safe from it?" – "Should I stay with my boyfriend or will our relationship never get better?"

Does the one who hears a prophecy made for him slacken in his striving and give up – and therefore experience the disaster that was foreseen and prophesied for him?

Or does the one who has heard the prophecy become reckless and therefore does not reach the good state that one has foreseen?

And: Does one always say everything that one has seen, or does one leave out or embellish some things?

Can one reliably distinguish one's perception of the future from one's own thinking and feeling, or do feelings and desires interfere with one's perceptions?

And what do you do when you foresee the course of an entire life?

These are all questions that cannot be answered in general, but to which only everyone can find his own point of view. The answers to these questions depend very much on one's own view of man and the world and life.

For a person with a very strong Hara, who lives carefree egoistically, it is no problem what the others make out of his prophecies. For a person with a very strong Third Eye, who looks primarily after the welfare of others, the consequences of one's own actions for others are an important issue – including the effect of one's own prophecies.

III 5.   The Benefits of Foresight

What can be the benefit of seeing the future, if the future is already fixed?

An able seer or seeress can see dangers and possibilities in the future and thereby help the community to which they belong to make decisions that lead to the disired state. Foreseeing a danger in the future and thereby avoiding it is then part of what is already fixed.

There is then, of course, the problem of the "time loop": the seer sees a disaster in the future and warns the community about it, which thereupon avoids it and therefore survives. Has the future been changed by the seer's warning? Has a new future been created by it?

In all cases known to me personally, quite simply what has been foreseen has come to pass.

In historical cases, which originate from cultures, in which Seer and Seeresses were a firmly established institution, often detailed things are predicted, which then also happend and on which humans relied. For example, the prophecy of a seeress, reported in the saga of Erik the Red, persuaded the Vikings in southern Greenland not to abandon their settlement, but to trust that in a short time they would again be successful in hunting and fishing, and that the epidemic that had just raged in their settlement would soon be over. Without this prophecy they would probably have sailed back to Iceland …

Can one, if one knows the future, strive for and achieve a better future than if one does not know the future? The only case for which I can affirm this for sure is the case that somebody has resigned and wants to give up – then a prophecy can give courage to the person concerned to continue striving and not to give up and finally reach a better state.

However, foreseeing the future in many cases upsets one's own world view so much that dealing with prophecies is not a simple matter. One can make actually only completely pragmatically in each situation the decision which seems the best at the moment.

And what does one do with the possibility to be able to look at the entire course of one's own remaining life including the own date of death? One can actually only make use of this possibility if one is willing to give up the perspective of the psyche and take the perspective of the soul – or in other words, to subordinate one's own psyche entirely to one's own soul. This is certainly a very essential step on one's path if one wants to become enlightened – or whatever one wants to call this spiritual goal. But it turns one's own life and above all one's own experience permanently and quite thoroughly upside down …

One can really only advise to first try out the future vision on a small scale and see how one experiences this and the effects of this knowledge on one's own life.

However, the vision of the future also has effects that are not at all connected with the knowledge about the future:

On the one hand, the experience of being able to foresee the future has a lasting effect on one's own view of the world.

On the other hand, practicing foresight promotes intuition and a sense of the best path that will take you where you want to go.

IV   The Effective Procedure of Seeing the Future

After all these considerations, the question naturally arises as to how to proceed most sensibly in order to see the future.

1. First of all, you can simply consult the tarot cards. This has the advantage that it is simple, and the disadvantage that one receives only a quality description as an answer, but no concrete description.

2. You may can supplement the Tarot cards by consulting the I Ching, which gives more concrete answers than the Tarot. When both are combined, the outlines usually become considerably clearer.

3. The next possible supplement is astrology, if the period one wants to look at is known and can be narrowed down so that at least the position of the slow planets Saturn, Uranus, Neptune and Pluto can be determined for this period.
From this you can get a further indication of quality, which you may combine with the answers of the Tarot and the I Ching.
If the future question refers to an individual, one can also compare the position of the four slow planets with the horoscope of the person concerned.

4. Indian astrology, in comparison with European astrology, gives much more concrete information, so that it is possible to take a step forward by using also indian astrology.

5. The simplest way to get direct and concrete perceptions of the future is to become quiet inside, to focus on the chosen topic in the future and then to see what impressions you get. This is a simple kind of dream journey.

6. If the question is important enough and you have the opportunity, you can also look into the future with several people and then compare the perceptions. From the things that all or at least several people have seen, you put together the basic statement, which is then supplemented by the things that only a few have seen. The information that only one person has seen is left out, because it could be just an association or similar.
If the picture found in this way agrees with the qualities described under points 1-5, one can be quite sure that the perceptions are correct. If one wants to combine both, one should first make the dream journey and then consult the oracles, in order not to be influenced by the oracle answer while doing the

dream journey.

7. You can also try out, which effect it has, if you imagine before the looking, that you send out a life force thread from your own solar plexus to the place and the time, about which you want to learn something. Possibly this facilitates the concentration and makes the perceptions clearer.

8. You can continue to make a family constellation with the future question. For this you define a place on the floor, where the desired information "stands", and then go yourself to this place and feel what you find there.

9. With the help of a dream journey or a constellation, one can make contact with a deceased person and ask him or her what will happen in the future.

10. You may also ask your own soul in a dream journey or meditation.

11. You may also ask a deity for an answer to your question on a dream journey or the like.

12. You may continue to travel to Chesed on the Kabbalistic Tree of Life, or to the Akashic Chronicle, to the Book of Destiny, i.e. to the central archive of the collective subconsciousness, which is known under different names in different systems.

13. It may also help to ask the question at the classical time for such questions, i.e. on New Year's Eve.

14. Maybe it also helps to become first completely quiet inwardly before looking into the future – to switch off all present pictures on the internal monitor, thus getting a "white projection surface" for the vision of the future, so to speak.

Of course, it is not necessary to make a complex process to look into the future - looking into the future can be quite simple … without any preparation simply like "remembering in the other direction" …
It is therefore useful to be clear about the purpose of the fourteen methods presented here.

One may, if one is dissatisfied with the effectiveness of one's own future vision, see what the reason for this is and then try out one of the aids for this problem in the following list. Some tools have multiple effects, so they appear several times in the following list.

1) Avoiding associations that have nothing to do with the topic:

a) Before looking at the future, go briefly into silence (deep sleep consciousness).

b) Checking the motivation for the upcoming future view.

c) Considering the feelings one associates with the future question.

d) Dream journey to Chesed, to the Akashic Chronicle or similar.

e) Questioning your own soul.

f) Questioning the ancestors.

g) Questioning a deity.

h) Sending a thread of life force (from the Solar Plexus or another Chakra) to the desired place and time in the future.

2. increase of concentration:

a) dream journey

b) family constellation

c) vision of the future on New Year's Eve

3. establishing a connection with the future or with the area where the future is easily accessible:

a) dream journey to Chesed, to the Akashic Chronicle or similar

b) Consultation of one's own soul

c) Questioning the ancestors

d) Questioning a deity

e) sending a life force thread to the desired place and time in the future.

4. <u>validation</u> of the results:

      a) use of the Tarot

      b) use of the I Ching

      c) use of European astrology (as far as possible)

      d) dream journey into the future to several persons

5. <u>concretization</u> of the quality descriptions obtained by oracles and the European astrology:

      a) use of Indian astrology

      b) dream journey

      c) dream journey with several persons

      d) constellation

As with just about everything, you are faced with the task of finding your own style, without which you will never be as effective as you could be. In finding this style (not only in terms of seeing the future), your own horoscope can be very helpful.

Good luck
and a prudent use of these possibilities!

English Books by Harry Eilenstein

- Living Magic (261 p.)
- The Synthesis of Physics and Magic (192 p.)
- Telepathy for Beginners (60 p.)
- Telepathy for Advanced Learners (52 p.)
- Telekinesis for Beginners (56 p.)
- Astral Projection for Beginners (60 p.)
- Prophecy for Beginners (60 p.)
- Invocations for Beginners (52 p.)
- Evocations for Beginners (62 p.)
- Auto-Movement for Beginners (60 p.)
- Elves for Beginners (56 p.)
- Hypnosis for Beginners (56 p.)
- Money Magic for Beginners (60 p.)
- Magic Objects for Beginners (64 p.)
- Shamanism for Beginners (52 p.)
- Number Symbolism for Beginners (64 p.)
- Crop Circles for Beginners (344 p.)

These books will be puplished soon:

- Life Force for Beginners
- Meditation for Beginners
- Kundalini for Beginners
- Chakra-Magic for Beginners
- Astrology for Beginners
- Ritual Magic for Beginners
- Mandalas for Beginners
- Love Magic for Beginners
- Magic Research for Beginners
- Self-awareness for Beginners
- Symbolism of Numbers for Beginners
- Language of the Moon – for Beginners
- Magic Chant for Beginners
- Da'ath-Magic for Beginners
- Feng Shui for Beginners
- Magic for Beginners – Anthology I
- Magic for Beginners – Anthology II
- Magic for Beginners – Anthology III
- Magic for Beginners – Anthology IV

Bücher von Harry Eilenstein

Religion allgemein
- Die sieben Schritte des Lebens (428 S.)
- Muttergöttin und Schamanen (168 S.)
- Göbekli Tepe (472 S.)
- Die Göttin von Göbekli Tepe (144 S.)
- Totempfähle (440 S.)
- Christus (60 S.)
- Dakini (80 S.)
- Vajra (76 S.)

Ägypten
- Hathor und Re 1: Götter und Mythen im Alten Ägypten (432 S.)
- Hathor und Re 2: Die altägyptische Religion – Ursprünge, Kult und Magie (396 S.)
- Isis (508 S.)

Indogermanen
- Die Entwicklung der indogermanischen Religionen (700 S.)
- Wurzeln und Zweige der indogermanischen Religion (224 S.)

Germanen
- Die Götter der Germanen (87 Bände – siehe nächste Seite)
- Odin (300 S.)

Kelten
- Cernunnos (690 S.)
- Taliesin (228 S.)
- Der Kessel von Gundestrup (220 S.)
- Der Chiemsee-Kessel (76)

Psychologie
- Über die Freude (100 S.)
- Das Geheimnis des inneren Friedens (252 S.)
- Das Beziehungsmandala (52 S.)
- Gefühle und ihre Verwandlungen (404 S.)
- einsgerichtet (140 S.)
- Liebe und Eigenständigkeit (216 S.)
- Von innerer Fülle zu äußerem Gedeihen (52 S.)

Heilung
- Die Symbolik der Krankheiten (76 S.)

Kunst
- Herz des Tanzes – Tanz des Herzens (160 S.)

Drama
- König Athelstan (104 S.)

Bücher von Harry Eilenstein

„Magie für Anfänger"

- Telepathie für Anfänger (60 S.)
- Telepathie für Fortgeschrittene (52 S.)
- Telekinese für Anfänger (52 S.)
- Lebenskraft für Anfänger (60 S.)
- Meditation für Anfänger (56 S.)
- Kundalini für Anfänger (100 S.)
- Hypnose für Anfänger (56 S.)
- Auto-Movement für Anfänger (56 S.)
- Chakra-Magie für Anfänger (148 S.)
- Astralreisen für Anfänger (56 S.)
- Astrologie für Anfänger (120 S.)
- Ritual-Magie für Anfänger (56 S.)
- Mandalas für Anfänger (68 S.)
- Geldzauber für Anfänger (56 S.)
- Liebeszauber für Anfänger (52 S.)
- Invokationen für Anfänger (52 S.)
- Evokationen für Anfänger (60 S.)
- Elfen für Anfänger (56 S.)
- Magie-Forschung für Anfänger (140 S.)
- Selbsterkenntnis für Anfänger (52 S.)
- Zahlensymbolik für Anfänger (60 S.)
- Die Sprache des Mondes – für Anfänger (116 S.)
- Zaubergesänge für Anfänger (100 S.)
- Zukunftschau für Anfänger (60 S.)
- Schamanismus für Anfänger (52 S.)
- Magische Gegenstände für Anfänger (68 S.)
- Da'ath-Magie für Anfänger (64 S.)
- Kornkreise für Anfänger (348 S.)
- Feng Shui für Anfänger (96 S.)
- Magie für Anfänger – Sammelband I (696 S.)
- Magie für Anfänger – Sammelband II (664 S.)
- Magie für Anfänger – Sammelband III (580 S.)

„Traumreisen"

- Traumreisen zu Heilpflanzen (700 S.)

Magie

- Handbuch für Zauberlehrlinge (408 S.)
- Tarot (104 S.)
- Physik und Magie (184 S.)
- Die Synthese von Physik und Magie (200S.)
- Die Magie-Formel (156 S.)
- Krafttiere – Tiergöttinnen – Tiertänze (112 S.)
- Schwitzhütten (524 S.)
- Mythen und Magie der Harfe (116 S.)
- Magie heute – Berichte aus der Praxis (288 S.)

Meditation

- Der Lebenskraftkörper (230 S.)
- Die Chakren (100 S.)
- Das Chakren-System mit den Nebenchakren (296 S.)
- Organe und Chakren (64 S.)
- Die platonischen Körper in den Chakren (156 S.)
- Meditation (140 S.)
- Drachenfeuer (124 S.)
- Kundalini I (676 S.)
- Reinkarnation (156 S.)
- einsgerichtet (140 S.)

Astrologie

- Astrologie (496 S.)
- Photo-Astrologie (428 S.)
- Die astrologischen Aspekte (88 S.)
- Horoskop und Seele (120 S.)

Kabbala

- Kursus der praktischen Kabbala (150 S.)
- Eltern der Erde (450 S.)
- Blüten des Lebensbaumes:
    - Die Struktur des kabbalistischen Lebensbaumes (370 S.)
    - Der kabbalistische Lebensbaum als Forschungshilfsmittel (580 S.)
    - Der kabbalistische Lebensbaum als spirituelle Landkarte (520 S.)

Die Themen der 87 Bände der Reihe „Die Götter der Germanen"